Sales Tactics-How to Earn a Living in Sales:

A Beginners Guide

Table Of Contents:

1) Brief Bio – Page 3
2) Reason for writing- Page 4
3) Getting the job- Page 8
4) Getting into character - Page 9
5) Educating & Familiarizing Yourself- Page 11
6) During the job – Page 22
    - Goals- Page 23
    - Outbound leads- Page 25
    - Inbound leads-Page 30
    - After the initial outbound/inbound call- Page 31
    - Generating your own leads- Page 33
7) Follow-ups & being organized- Page 37
8) Emails- Page 42
9) Calls- Page 44
10) Voicemails & gatekeepers- Page 47
11) Summation- Page 49
12) Appendices- Page 50

Brief bio

Nicholas Vicale is 34 years old and lives with his Wife, Alisa, and their 2 year old Siberian husky, Monroe, in East Patchogue, NY. Nicholas enjoys reading Stephen King, jogging, and playing basketball. He has been in sales for over 12 years in various industries that include mortgages, retail, energy and gas, commercial loans and business equipment financing. His experience in these fields include (but are not limited to) telemarketing, implementing marketing campaigns, inside sales, appointment setting, outside sales, administration, processing, and underwriting. During Nicholas' time selling business loans he helped start a funding company previously called *"Prime Funding Source"*. Through hard work and dedication he became a partner before making the jump into Equipment Financing where he has been ever since. Nicholas attended Oneonta State receiving his BS in Mathematics and also received his MBA in marketing at Stony Brook University. Special thank you to his sister, Michelle, for her support, guidance, and help with this project.

Reason for writing

I remember when I was in high school, or even college for that matter, I had no idea what I wanted to do for a living. When I was growing up I wanted to play in the NBA, but realized when I stopped growing in 7th grade, that it would not be possible. I ended up playing Division 3 college ball, however, I ultimately fell short of my lofty goal. The only thing I knew was that I wanted a fulfilling career that compensated me for my efforts and would end up being financially rewarding.

Going into college I chose Math as my major. This was because I wanted to maximize my fun but minimize my stress as math came very easy for me.

When I graduated undergrad I STILL had no clue as to what I was going to do with my life. I bounced around a lot. I worked in restaurants, diners, pizzerias, construction, and finally got my first sales job selling mortgages and refinances. At the ripe age of 23 I found a job selling home mortgages and because of my math background, learned the total scope of the financing part of the business faster than most others.

I fell in love with sales; the cushy office, the independence of being your own boss, the money that had no ceiling, unlimited potential, the people...everything. This particular job was 100% commission (some sales jobs pay 100% commission, some pay small salary high commission, and some pay you great salary low commission). With commission jobs, If you didn't work you didn't get paid, or you got paid but didn't like the monetary amount of your check. Obviously if you didn't get paid for more than a few weeks then you should just quit and save the sales manager the hassle of firing you.

When I walked into that place and saw what a handful of people were making I knew I wanted to do this for a long time. You can tell who was successful and who wasn't. The cars they drove, clothes they wore, their attitude and professionalism in the office, the hunger they showed to keep dialing even after a big closing to keep riding that "good wave" of fortune. Sales also played into my competitive nature from sports. I would have internal motivation to meet my own goals whether it was sales, metrics, or financial goals, and I had external goals to beat certain sales reps within the office and amongst my team.

Now, not everyone is the "sales-y" type, if there is such a thing. I never thought of myself as being persuasive or a "seller". I consider myself smart, I work hard, and I am extremely organized. I used those strengths and proved that I can be decent at sales right away. I eventually worked on my weaknesses and that's when I elevated my sales career to the new level.

I have always made a good living in sales. I was never one to lead the office in revenue or commission; however, I was always consistent and even cracked a 6 figure income (which I think is always an initial goal of a sales rep).

The main reason I am writing this booklet is because I feel anyone that is looking for a rewarding career, has a good head on their shoulders, and is determined to make money can benefit and excel in a sales environment. I want to clear the air with all the negative connotations that are associated with sales and provide a small guide based on my experiences to help others succeed in a sales environment.

The following pages can guide anyone to making a living in sales and how you should be treating your desk, office, or cubicle as your own little business. I know when people hear the words "sales" or "cold calling" they get scared and apprehensive. Honestly, all that sales means is that you are your own business owner. Your finances are in your own hands and you own your cubicle, office, or wherever you work out of. For this guide I have not done any extra research or included any quotes from famous sales "gurus". The following is all firsthand knowledge and experiences that I encountered during my career which I find very helpful. If you read this and take the information in, along with learning from your colleagues and superiors during on the job training, then you can make a good living doing sales.

Getting the job

First thing, you have to land a job. When I first got into sales I didn't really think much of the interview process or what service/product the company was providing or selling to their customers. However, if you are new to sales it may be more beneficial to find a company that provides a product or service you believe in. It's always easier to come off enthusiastic or positive when the product you are offering holds benefits and values you believe in and can get behind. However, no matter what you sell, even if you do not believe in your product and your job merely provides a paycheck, you need to treat your position as a potential career, not a job.

Sales is a revolving door as many reps bounce from place to place within an industry, or they may bounce from industry to industry. Reps usually do this in order to find a place where they feel they can make money whether it is products offered, pay structure, compensation/bonus plans, travel requirements, etc. So whether you want to stay there, or not, you need to treat it as a career in order to maximize your financial potential.

Getting into Character and Assuming the Role

When I start, I always dress the part. I never went to work casual or disheveled. I wanted to convey success from day one. I am not saying you need to have a three piece suit with cufflinks and tie clips. But I would always be in dress pants, button down shirt (sometimes with tie) or polo shirt with dress shoes. I wanted to feel like I was working. Even when I work from home, I would still take the time to shave, get dressed, make my cup of coffee, and sit in my home office to feel like I am at work and I am working to make money.

Another thing I do (along the lines of dressing the part) is acting the part. I would get into character. Even if you don't have the answer to everything or you are not an expert in your field, I would act like I was an expert: Play the role. A lot of sales today isn't done face to face. It's through emails, phones, texting, social media etc. That gives you the ability to be who you want, and what you should want is to be an expert. Always exude confidence on the phone and in your writing correspondence. If you don't know something, you are allowed to say you don't know and you will find out. Clients/customers are coming to you to fulfill a need, so they need to be confident they are dealing with an expert and someone that can help them. When speaking on the phone you need to be enthused, honest, and empathetic. Keep in mind sales isn't necessarily always "hard" selling; nowadays it is more of a consulting role. Everyone has answers to questions at the swipe of an I-pad or smart phone, so your job is to consult them in a manner where you convey your value and how you can help them accomplish their end goal.

One huge aspect of sales is being positive and staying in the right mind set. You will hear the word "no" a lot more often than hearing the word "yes". Ninety-five percent of your solicitation from emails or left messages won't even receive a response. You can't let that break you. You have to stay enthused and positive and realize any type of sales is a numbers game. The more you put yourself out there, the more positive responses you will receive, and the more potential deals you will ultimately get.

Educating & Familiarizing Yourself

Whenever I walk into a new sales role my goal is to learn right away. Not just the product/service, but the overall sales cycle and process, the industry, and the players in the industry like industry competitors and other market leaders. The only way you can truly sell and consult your clients is to know your industry and be truly confident.

To start, I would listen to co-workers and take notes right away. I would sit in on their calls and listen to key phrases, rebuttals, and sales pitches and write them down. Every night after work I would take my notebook and type those notes and then save onto my zip drive or USB. I would then print out in small font (cheat sheets should not be longer than 2 pages) and take it with me every day. I would read it on the train, in the parking lot at lunch, or even on the bowl (sorry for the mental picture). Anyway, that is how I would learn fast and efficiently. The quicker you know what you are talking about in regards to your product/service and the overall process, the quicker you can sell and make money.

Do not be afraid to ask questions. If you field a call, or make a call, and a client asks you something you don't know, find out that answer for them and make a note to yourself so you won't have to ask that question again. The answers to the questions should automatically go onto your cheat sheet as well. A lot of people are scared to ask questions, however management doesn't see this as a sign of not being smart or a sign of weakness. If they are good managers, they will see this as a sign that you take your job seriously, you are willing to learn, and want to make the effort to learn.

In addition, I shouldn't have to state this but, you should always go to work TO WORK. Depending on the industry, the lead sources and flow, the clientele and so on and so forth, sales reps can experience lag times or prolonged downtime. Use this time to work on another aspect of your job. You can't make money in sales if you don't put in the effort. On down times I studied my notes to learn my job and market. I liked to practice my pitch and rebuttals with co-workers and even to myself in a mirror or silently. I found myself googling potential customers (this was for commercial sales not residential) and cold calling or emailing my own, self-generated leads from online searches. The point is, don't use down time to relax. Relaxing is the "cancer" of a sales rep. That is what lunch is for. That is what HOME is for. When you are at work everything you do should create a potential output for increasing your personal stream of revenue.

Another great thing to do when you start out at a new place is to ask for old leads to solicit. I like doing this for a variety of different reasons:

>1) It shows initiative that you want to get out there and make it happen.

>2) It allows you to practice your pitch and your rebuttals and work the kinks out of your selling style i.e; pitch, tone, spacing of words etc.

>3) it allows you to do the above reason without incurring the company any marketing dollars for new leads.

Also, you never know what can transpire with old leads. Sometimes it is all about timing and a lead that said "no" nine times before might be in the right place or situation to say "yes" during your call.

Another good practice when starting out in a sales position is to let people in your circle know what you do. You can start with family and friends. A lot of people aren't comfortable selling to family and friends. If that is you, don't sell to them. Just tell them what you do and if they ask questions, answer them. Maybe they are interested in hearing more about your products or services. Maybe they know someone outside of your personal circle that can use your products or services. The point is you never know. To go along with this concept, I always used to post on social media about my new position. Whether it be Facebook, Twitter, or LinkedIn, I would post about what I currently do or products I offer with a "message me if interested" line. You would be surprised how many positive responses you get from that simple task. If you have 250 friends on Facebook and 1 person shares your post then you also have access to that person's circle of friends. It's an easy way to get some free passive advertising for yourself.

Also, try joining groups within your industry. LinkedIn is perfect for this as well. If you are selling business loans you can join a multitude of groups where you think you may be able to reach a person that can use your product or service.

When I started a new industry the first thing I did was update my LinkedIn with a brief description of what I currently do as well as a brief bio about my new company. Within weeks I had many Linked IN friends message me to see if I can help their client, inquired about my rates, or asking for a certain type of equipment preference. Again, this is another easy way you may be able to get a few deals in without working your company's leads.

Now, once you get acclimated and educated on the product or service you need to learn your sales pitch and rebuttals. I found it very helpful to do a couple of things. First, I would type up each pitch on my own time as previously stated. I would have an elevator pitch (a quick 20 second pitch in case the person on the other end of the phone was rushing me or I knew I had a short period of time to get my point across). I would have my main opening pitch and certain rebuttals typed for the most prominent questions/objections I saw while shadowing a fellow colleague during my training period.

Once I had everything typed, I would re-read it whenever I had time. I wanted it embedded in my mind. Too many novices make calls reading from their script. This is a mistake. If you do that you come across as a robot; very monotone. If you add infliction while still reading, you may come across fake. I wanted to know the main points of the script so well that I didn't need to state it verbatim. I wanted to have each call sound different as a normal conversation does while my main points are being included. I would practice in the mirror or even talk aloud while driving on my way to work. I would call friends or family and ask for feedback. I did whatever I could in order to hone in on my "selling" skills.

Learning your pitch and how to speak to clients is very important; however, your education shouldn't stop there. Learning the whole sales-cycle is very important. Depending on your product or service, the customer experience doesn't end with you making the sale, or having them sign your contract. My specific role might end and I may pass the "baton" to another department to wrap things up, however, I wanted to learn every aspect of my company. The more you know about the whole process, the more you sound like an expert in your field. You are then able to consult and guide your client with facts and knowledge while setting up your clients expectations to give them a clear map of where they will travel from point A to point Z within your organization. Many reps don't go this far. This will help distinguish you from the rest. If reps don't see it impacting their sales numbers or bottom line right away they won't do it. However, some clients need that type of "hand-holding" from the reps they deal with and if you go the full "ten yards" with them they are more apt to come back and even refer you some new contacts.

In addition to learning the "ins and outs" of your company, a sales rep should also learn about their competition and the industry as a whole. For instance, I had a client that was looking for a $100,000 working capital loan. I provided them with an approval and structure and he came back saying he got a better offer elsewhere. I asked him for the name of the lender and he provided me with that name. I instantly knew how they hooked him. I told him I was familiar with that company as I used to do business with them. I expressed to him that by me working for a leading broker agency in this field we have many strong relationships with banks/lenders that allow us to offer lower rates and special programs that business owners might not qualify for on their own (this was a partially true statement but we did provide good services and helped the owners we worked with find what they needed) and it allows me to find the best deal possible to fit their needs.

I continued my rebuttal and I asked him to find the pages of the documents that deal with fees. This particular company charges an upfront fee and an origination fee (taken out of the proceeds of the loan) so he wasn't getting anywhere near $100,000. On top of that, my offer, while slightly more expensive, had a structure that worked well with the owners cash flow. I asked him to tell me the terms on his contract and he stated he thought it was a 12 month short term loan. I did the numbers with him and stated that this bank doesn't offer more than 9 month notes. If they hold back 20% of your credit card sales every time you batch-out, then you are estimated to pay this off in 8.5-9 months based on your processing numbers from last year. So my 11 month loan at a higher interest rate was actually more cost effective in terms of interest per month than his expected 9 month loan. He thanked me for the information and said he would get back to me; which he did 1 hour later by emailing me my company's signed documents.

Now, instances like this aren't always cut and dry, but the more you know about your competitions offerings, sales tactics, prices, and promotions etc., the more ammunition you have to sell the value and benefit of the product/service and company in the best way possible. Even if you charge slightly more, people will pay more for more expected value, convenience, and ease and if they feel they trust the person on the other end of the phone/email.

Learning the industry as a whole is SO beneficial. Knowing if there are rules and regulations changing down the road such as: prime rates going up, the DOW going down, and if marketable securities will take a hit are all things you need to know. From a client's POV, they realize they are dealing with someone extremely knowledgeable who can provide them with accuracy and certainty in an ever-changing environment.

There is no greater teacher than experience. The more you do something, the more comfortable you get and the more second nature it becomes. At first, you might be scared to make an outbound call to a client, however, the more calls you make and the more you hear the word "no" or phrases such as "stop calling," and "take me off your list," you come to actually crave those words. That is called closure! You cross that prospect off your list and you move on to other potential money making calls.

Truth be told, I actually like hearing "no" more than I like hearing "can you call me back "when you instinctively know they don't want a call back and they don't sound genuine about it. I like closure; whether it is "YES" or "NO". With that being said, yes, experience is a great teacher. However, in sales I believe failing is an even better teacher. Most people are afraid of failure when they start out. They don't want to blow the sales call when a client finally answers. They don't want to sound stupid if they don't know the answer. You (especially as a novice) should embrace failures. Fail and then review why you failed. Did you fumble your words? If so, practice your pitch. Did you not know an answer to a question the client posed? If yes, then study your product or services offered. Did you make the mistake of over-talking? If so, next time state your pitch and take a breath and let the client speak. No one is perfect. Not one millionaire is 100% successful on sales calls. In fact, they are probably less than 5% successful on sales calls. But the difference is they make a ton of calls and they make the most out of the positive 5%.

You are not the only one that makes mistakes. In sales meetings bring up your failures and see if anyone has any feedback to share. Other sales reps probably will bring up their own mistakes. This is a great time to learn from others without having to make the same mistakes yourself. Sometimes sharing "old war stories" is a great way to go over the mistakes made, rebuttals that should have been said, closing techniques, and so on and so forth.

One last thing I want to mention about starting out in sales is something I already briefly touched upon. Stay positive and in character. Your mental state is very important. If you are depressed or stressed because you need the sale to close for financial reasons, the clients can sense that. It is the "the smell" of desperation. Stay happy, motivated, empathetic, and consult your client. Be honest and frank while selling your value and your company's value. You will have to do this over and over again and will be rejected over and over again, however, you need to keep chin up and "smile and dial" or "dial for dollars." Always dress professionally. The better you dress, the better you feel. If you shave, and smell good, and look the part, you will be more confident. This confidence will be heard through the other line of the call.

During the Job

For the next few sections I will not provide actual pitches, sequences of conversations, or acronyms like ABC (always be closing). I will let you know how I handle certain situations I have seen throughout my days as a sales rep. I'll go into how to organize your day, how to handle different leads (like inbound and outbound calls), how to generate your own leads, and how to come up with your own account entry strategies. This is a guideline that is built upon experience.

GOALS

The first important thing is to set goals for yourself. Now, your company might outline a certain matrix for you to follow like making 100 calls a day, receiving one application a day, and one closing a week. However, you should set your own goals to follow. I personally like to back into a salary I want to make. I will use working capital loans as an example. I wanted to make $75,000 a year in my second year. The average deal size was $25,000 and the average commission to our company was 5% ($1250). My split would be 30% of that ($375). My salary at that time was $30,000, so I needed to make $45,000 in commission with my average ticket being $375. This meant I had to close 120 deals a year which translates to 10 deals a month or 2 deals a week.

My company had the following metric. For every deal closed you had to submit 5 deals. So if I wanted to close two a week, I needed to get 10 deals submitted per week. For every 15 applications filled out there would be a submission. So I needed 50 applications a week (or ten a day) in order to get the submissions I needed to close the deals I needed to close (Appendix E).

Now sometimes you close less than what your goal was and you make more, and sometimes you close more than your goal and you make less. It depends on the deal size, order size if you sell products, bonus structure, and commission structure etc. Nonetheless, if you establish what is needed to reach your financial goal, then you have a blueprint and can plan on what you need to do every hour of every day.

Outbound Leads

Handling outbound Leads is basically "dialing for dollars". There is a certain mindset when you are constantly dialing outbound calls all day long. If you are lucky, you will work in a place that has an automatic dialer. With an automatic dialer, you just put your headset on sit at your desk and make your pitch whenever someone picks up the line. Once you or the other person hangs up, the dialer then finds you another lead on the other end of the line. The dialer is a great tool for making over a hundred or so calls a day. It definitely can get monotonous, but you need to remember any one of these calls can turn into a deal and any one deal can turn into commission. I loved getting on the dialer.

The key to getting on the dialer is to make sure you give yourself ample time to get into rhythm. It is easy to sit on there for 20-30 minutes and not even make 1 solid pitch or have a conversation. You can get hung up on, get cut off and then hung up on, or even get into the first few lines of your pitch and then here the dreaded "not interested, take me of your list." This can definitely affect your positive mindset and get boring at times. You must stay the course. I would stay on the dialer until I got an actual solid lead/deal or filled out an application from it. Once that takes place I would allow myself a brief break but then get right back on the dialer. Some sales organizations break their day up to soliciting for new leads/deals and the other half handling business that was already converted to deals. If that is the case for your job, then you have a finite time each day to get new business. So you must continue to get on the dialer and stay the course.

I spoke briefly about pitches and rebuttals. This is where they come in to play. You will have your main pitch down packed. You may even have your rebuttals memorized for 90% of the questions/concerns that can occur. However, most sales reps run into problems when they can't get into their pitch from the get-go. Remember, when you are cold calling or even calling interested (warm) leads, you may be interrupting the day of the other person on the line. These leads are people who have their own lives, own issues, and own job problems and family problems they need to overcome. You simply may be bothering them. You can hear it in their voice; "IM NOT INTERESTED," "NO THANKS," "CLICK," "What do you want? Make it quick." In these cases you need to have a quick 10-20 second elevator pitch where you can get your reason for calling across and maybe peak their interest for a continued conversation or worse case a better time to call back.

I mentioned getting into rhythm but another good tip when "dialing for dollars" or "pounding the phones" is to stand up when you get a person on the line. When you stand up and talk your diaphragm is open and you sound better on the phone. Your confidence and excitement is conveyed in the correct tone and pitch. It also breaks the long session of just sitting there for hours straight and then possibly sounding like the dreaded robot we ,as sales, people do not want to fall into.

When that amazing, adrenaline pumping time comes when you do get a person picking up the phone and they are interested and they have time to chat ("the perfect storm" of a sales call) you need to handle with care. Much like fishing (I have no idea I never fish but I understand the concept), you need to give the fish some slack on the line to tire out and reel them in slowly and then give more slack to the line and reel in slowly again. This tires the fish out to the point where you eventually have the fish on the boat and you now have dinner on the table. It is the same when speaking to the client. You made your pitch, they are interested in talking, so now what do you do? Most sales organizations have a brief questionnaire/ application that they can take over the phone to qualify a person to see if they can be approved (if you are selling loans) or to even give you selling points for a future close (if the questionnaire has to do with selling walk-in bath tubs and they mention they have back ache, now you have a benefit of the product that addresses that persons needs directly). When you ask them questions, do not rattle off 10 questions straight. Get them talking about each answer.

"Have you ever had a bankruptcy?"

"Yes"

"ugh, I know those are horrible to deal with, How did it work out"

"It was a grueling process, credit dropped"

"I hear you on that; I deal with a lot of clients with similar situations. You mentioned your credit dropped, did you seek credit repair professionals since then or did you try to build it up on your own?"

From my first question I had established a dialogue. I took a simple "yes or no" question that would take someone 1 second to answer turned it into a 3-5 minute conversation. This is important because the more you speak to that person in a caring, empathetic, and professional manner the more you build trust and rapport with that client.

When you are in the middle of an engaging conversation during a sales call the most important thing to do (besides asking questions) is listening to them and taking notes. Again, certain answers may help you close the client down the line. They may give certain key pieces of information you can use to get them to purchase or product or use your service because you linked a benefit of your product/service to their specific need. Write down everything they say that is applicable.

Most sales organizations have a CRM (customer relationship management) system where it helps the reps organize their leads, shows their whole book of business and has areas where they can type notes about each client. I would always write on paper first. I didn't want the client to hear me typing over the phone. I would jot down short hand notes during the conversation and then take the time after the call to input it in my CRM system. Please see Appendix C and D which goes into some detail on Selling and 3 call approach.

Inbound Leads

If you are lucky enough to work for an organization that has a strong marketing campaign and they have a website that generates call ins or that have ads on TVs or radio that generate call-ins, then you want to work on these inbound call campaigns. Inbound calls are the "Primetime" leads. These are calls from people already interested in what you are selling and providing. They either surfed the internet looking for a website they trusted, or they heard the advertisement on whatever medium they were listening to. For these calls you do not have to be in "Bull Dog" sales mode. I find that for these calls it is always best to be a consultant and an expert. They are calling to learn more, so inform and instruct them. Ask if they have certain questions and provide expertise knowledge they are seeking. Ask for their emails and send them brochures, literature, schedule follow-up "Consultation calls". You pretty much have the driver's seat during these calls, but sometimes it is better to just be a passenger during the call. As I said, they are calling because they want what you are selling and they want information. Just consult them to the goal line, but don't give them a reason not to buy.

After the Initial Inbound/Outbound Call

Whenever I speak to a first time lead, whether it is the first time I connect on an outbound dial or whether it is an inbound lead, I find it very helpful to send an email to the client with some information.

The information can be anything from thanking them for taking the time to speak and giving them all your contact information, or attaching PDF's or pamphlets/literature explaining your products or services for them to review at their leisure. I find this helps a lot with follow-up calls/emails (which we will get into later). This gives you a reason to email or call them to touch base to see if they had any questions on what you sent them after your initial call.

Also, you can show the professionalism of your company by providing links to your website, your LinkedIn profile, or even a website that provides customer testimonials similar to Glassdoor. The more information you can provide the customer upfront, the easier it is to establish a rapport with that client and the easier it is for them to remember you once you do your follow-up soliciting.

Let me also add that people in sales, as well as many other fields, believe in the 80/20 principle in which 80% of your business comes from 20% of your clients. These would be your A-tier clients. A-tier clients are usually the bigger companies that can afford more purchases or services, and come back for repeat business and transactions. The other 20% of your business comes from your B-Tier and C-Tier clients.

However, do not treat customers any differently than you would you're A-tier clients. Treat every client as if they are an A-Tier client. You never know what the future can bring. Some B-Tier clients can transform their business and grow in scale and scope and down the line may become an A-Tier client for your book of business.

Generating Your Own Leads

Relying on the outbound call sheets, dialers and inbound calls provided by your organization should only be about 75% of your lead stream. The other 25% should be generated by you. Sales reps are given all the tools to find deals on their own time or by their own accord. Some organizations even give higher commissions for self-generated deals. There are lots of different routes one can go about this and a few of them I already touched upon.

1) Tell family and friends what you do- I spoke about this earlier.
2) Post to social media- LinkedIN , Facebook, Twitter, about what you do, post about recent transactions that closed and how you overcame obstacles to get the deal across the finish line. Someone in the same situation may see that post and decide to give you a try.
3) Referrals are one of the easiest ways to get a new deal with built in trust. Whenever I close a deal with a client and I know they had a good experience from "start to finish" I simply ask them, "Do you know anyone in your circle that may need my services/product?". They may know family

members or friends in the same situation. If you provide commercial services they may even know business owners who may need your services. Business owners meet at community events and conventions. They love talking about their "baby", their business. Even if they do not know of anyone off the top of their head, they may run across someone in the near future who needs your help. A referral may have their defensive walls down as they will trust you because they know of a firsthand testimonial. If you do get a referral from a client, it may be a good idea to send that client a gift card, or even a thank you card showing your appreciation to them. This may get them thinking of more people they can send your way as they know you appreciate your relationship with them even after your initial transaction with that client is over.

4) Business cards- A lot of new sales reps think it is so important for their organization to get them business cards right away. 95% of the time the box of cards will stay in the desk or on top of the desk to never be used. I made this mistake early in my career as well. I thought it was "cool" to have my own business card, but when I got

them I didn't know what to do with them and they ultimately ended up being an expense my company never got any returns on. Now, I know better. I have a few business cards in my wallet, a few at the office, a few in my car, and at home. Below is a few things to do with your business cards

    a. Keeping a few in your wallet- similarly to telling people in your circle of friends and family what you do, you should also try to engage in conversation wherever you are. If you are in a bar or restaurant waiting for a table or any situation where you strike up conversation with people about your careers, feel free to hand them your card just in case they know anyone. This is why I also keep some in my car so I can fill-up my wallet when need be.

    b. Keeping a few at my desk allows me to pass out cards to any clients that walk into our location. Give them a couple for themselves and a couple of extras for people they may know.

c. Go to community networking events- you can see these posted on LinkedIn or in your local papers. Networking events are perfect to solicit yourself and talk about what you do. Take cards of others and in return hand yours out. You never know, you may even develop a business relationship with a sales rep in a different industry that may deal with clients who also need your services. You can work out referral programs between the two of you and strike a nice working relationship with someone outside of your sales organization.

d. Conventions- similar to networking events you can also check for conventions that are specific to your industry. These may be more gratifying as the vendors or the spectators walking the floor are guaranteed to be in the same field or involved in the same industry as you.

FOLLOWUPS and BEING ORANIZED

Once you have spoken to someone and qualified them as a solid potential lead and someone who is definitively interested in your products or service, you now need to follow-up with them until they are ready to purchase or sign your contracts. Ninety-nine percent of sales is the follow-up. Closing a deal on the first call is extremely rare and unheard of. Being extremely organized helps with secondary and tertiary follow-ups necessary to get the deal in. First, let us cover being organized

Every sales rep will be equipped with their CRM system as well as whatever email platform the company uses (I have always had Microsoft outlook). A sales rep should always ask how to use some of the key functionalities of these platforms and email systems. They are all equipped to assist you on your day to day, week to week, and month to month activities. A lot of CRM systems allow you to take effective notes, schedule callbacks, send out emails, and create email templates among others. These functionalities should be learned during a reps' beginning stages. This way when a rep starts gathering qualified leads they can effectively call back and engage these leads until they convert them to closings and commission checks.

I have always liked using outlook for my future planning. Some key things to learn to use here are:

1) Sending yourself future emails- Sometimes you just want a reminder and you can set yourself a reminder by sending an email to yourself for a future date. On that date, you will receive an email with whatever note you typed in the body of the email.
2) Utilizing the calendar- there is a calendar section in most emails where you can organize tasks daily or set up future tasks down the road.
3) You can flag certain emails- Some reps get dozens, if not hundreds, of e-mails a day. The key is to prioritize. I would answer emails as they come in, but if they didn't require immediate attention I would red flag them. You can flag them for "today," "tomorrow," "next week," and so on. I would make sure I would circle back to the "today" emails and if I had time even get a head start on "tomorrow". This function is extremely helpful when you are in an organization that sends a lot of internal emails.
4) Setting up folders in Outlook- As a sales rep you will receive tons of emails regarding deals in various stages of

the funding cycle including applications submitted, approved deals , documents sent out to be signed, and documents signed waiting to fund. I find it very helpful to organize your emails into folders so you can easily search for certain deals. The main point of this is to keep your inbox clean. Your inbox should be your targeted goals for the day requiring responses. Any correspondence outside of that can be divvied up into the applicable folders (Appendix F).

5) There are many more functionalities an email system can provide , however, it is up to the sales rep to learn the additional uses.

In addition to the CRM systems and the email systems I just mentioned, I also did things on my own that most reps and colleagues didn't do. I was always scared of dropping the ball and "leaving money on the table" by missing a follow-up or not calling someone back in a good time period and being too late. Every evening I would set up my "hit list" for the following day. This "hit list" was everything I wanted to do and everything I should do in regards to deals and leads that were already in my pipeline. I would set up my hit list in order of importance. For example, most sales in finance have familiar milestones: 1) APP IN -you get an signed and completed application with a financial package (tax returns, pay stubs, bank statements etc.) from a potential client looking to get approved, 2) Submission for approval: you submit that applicant to the lenders you deal with or you submit to your own internal credit department. 3) Approval- you have an approval you need to sell, 4) Documents- they want to move forward with your offer so you sent out documentation to be signed, 5) Docs IN- they sign and returned your documents and the back end department works to close the deal and 6) Funding/Commission.

I would go through all my deals at each stage and set up my "hit list" accordingly. Below is an example of the "Hit list" . I also included a Mock Schedule in Appendix B:

1) Docs IN (most important to me because that is my next commission check)
    a. Company "A"- Funding department needs borrower to resign page 6 of the documents and provide driver's license. Get this stuff so we can close.
    b. Company "B"- underwriters can't get a hold of borrower for the closing call, get in touch.

2) Documents out:

   a. Company "C"- docs have been out for a week, if borrower moving forward, do they have questions? Get a hold of them

3) Approval:

   a. Company "D"- new offer on table- call and go over his options

   b. Company "E"- didn't like my first offer, I need to tweak offer with underwriting and present a new offer if there is one.

4) Application IN:

   a. Company "F"- have the application but I can't submit. Missing other financial information.

Now, you have your hit list! What do you do with it? How do you follow-up?

E-MAILS

There are multiple ways for a rep to follow-up with a client or a potential lead. I - initially follow-up with an email. I do this for a couple of reasons: 1) like to carefully articulate what I want to say and 2) emailing gives me a reason to then call them if they do not respond within a day. It is always best to get the client or lead on the phone to go over offers or hash things out, however, sometimes it is also better to schedule a call with the client to assure you both have time to speak and go over the full transaction. I like to keep my emails brief, but detailed as well as ask the best time to connect.

Another reason I also like using emails for an initial follow-up is because it allows me to type up generic templates and then "e-mail blast" certain leads. I will make a template for "cold leads," "touching base" templates, "following up on open stipulations" templates, "following up on contracts" templates, and so on and so forth. I will then take these templates and copy and paste them while personalizing for that specific client before I send. This allows me to follow-up, or touch base on a variety of topics and also allows me to blast through a list of follow-ups efficiently and quickly for numerous prospects or clients.

I try to make a rule to never follow-up on an email with another email. It is always better to call after my initial email.

Calls:

Whenever I follow-up via call I always grab the file I already have on the client. I might have certain notes that I jotted down to help reconnect with that client.

"Hey Bill, its Nick from _____, how are you? How was your trip to Massachusetts? "

As previously mentioned, it's important to take notes and build rapport with the client. You are probably not the only one calling this person looking to sell them something or offer your services to them. So, when you are following up for either additional information or signed documents, you need to re-affirm who you are and reconnect with the client to show you care and you listened.

After you connect with the client, I keep it brief and to jump over any obstacle that they throw in my way.

"Bill, did you decide on whether or not you wanted to move forward with that approval from my bank?"

No, I am still thinking it over with my wife

"Ok, I understand. Yes, it is a big decision. Do you or your wife have any questions in regards to the offer? Maybe, its best we schedule a conference call to go over the approval structure and terms together? Is there a time we can all connect?"

If they made their decision to not move forward with you then, ask WHY? Let them tell you why they are going with someone else or why they aren't interested. A lot of times, they just don't understand fully the term of your offering or they are moving forward with some other company that undercut you.

"I am sorry that this didn't work out for you. Is there any particular reason you aren't moving forward with this? Let me know because if there is anything I can do on my end I will try to do so. I have no problem "rolling up my sleeves" and "going to bat" for you if it is in the realm of possibility of meeting your needs."

Again, these aren't follow-up pitches to live by. I am in the financial sales industry so we follow-up every step of the way. Maybe they sent an application but we still need tax returns to submit for approval. The follow-up does not need to be scripted. You simply ask for what is missing. Follow-ups concerning contracts/documents are more tricky and you will rely on your corporate training and wisdom of your supervisors and colleagues for the best way to go about things.

I promised I wouldn't include pitches in this pamphlet however, I am including a list of top 20 "closings" (Appendix A). You will learn how to close a potential client when selling your product or services from your company. I always found it interesting to see how you can close a client a variety of different ways. All clients are not the same and there is no "cookie-cutter" way to go, so it is the sales-reps jobs to learn from their training and supervisors while learning other strategies on their own to incorporate into their own repertoire. You can find the list of closings at the end of this pamphlet.

Gatekeepers/Voicemails:

You will always run into "Gatekeepers" when tracking down your commercial clients. By "Gatekeepers" I mean secretaries, assistants, or co-workers of your potential client who weed out solicitation efforts to not waste their bosses/co-workers time. When I speak to them I automatically let them know that I was already dealing with this person and that I have prior business that needs to be discussed.

"Hi Is Bill available"

"Who is this?"

"Its Nick from_____"

"Oh, Sorry, he is not interested"

"Really? I just spoke to him last week and he sent me some paperwork that I needed. I was following up for the missing items to complete his file? "

"I am sorry, we get so many sales calls. Who did you say you were with?"

"Not a problem, I am with _____. I recently spoke to Bill and he advised me he will be undertaking a project and was looking for some solutions to get everything across the finish line. He told me to try him back in a week"

Now, if they transfer me and I have to leave a voicemail my goal is to leave an engaging voicemail and to cover certain things to help ensure a call back.

In every voicemail I articulate who I am, establish some type of reconnection, why I am calling, and best number or email to reach me at.

"Hi Bill, its Nick from_____. I hope you had a nice long relaxing weekend. We spoke last week in regards to financing for your upcoming marketing campaign. I just wanted to follow-up with you to see if you had any questions on the application I sent you or the paperwork that we would need to vet the file. Feel free to call me at 555-555-5555 or email me at nvicale@domain.com in case you need anything before submitting your paperwork. I look forward to assisting you with this. Have a great day, talk to you soon"

Summation:

The purpose of this was not to show you that sales is easy or a cushy job. In fact, sales can be very stressful and full of ups and downs. It is a roller coaster of emotion. One month you can feel on top of the world and have a nice commission check to show for it. The next month you can be on the "hot seat" and have nothing to show for your efforts besides an upset sales manager. However, if you treat your job as a career and really put in the effort, then there is no reason why you can't succeed and make a living in sales.

You may not be a sales export or the best on the phone, but always put in the effort. Study your products, study your competitors, and be organized. Your clients will respect you for that. Be transparent and honest with them. Even if you don't make that sale chances are, if you are honest and empathetic, they will remember you and may give you business down the road.

I hope you found this brief guide helpful. It was fun for me to write and it actually re-invigorated me in my own career. Good Luck in your sales job and remember to be humble, continue learning, and be hungry!

Appendix A:

My Favorite 20 Closing Techniques:

1) Affordable Close- ensuring them and showing them they can afford your offer by budgeting their expenses and income

2) Ask the manager close- use your manager to offer "discounts" and help close

3) Balance sheet close- going over pros and cons

4) Compliment Close- flatter them into submission

5) Conditional close- link closure to resolving an issue or objection

6) Daily cost close- reduce the cost to a daily amount

7) Demonstration Close- show them how it works

8) Economic Close- help them pay less than they currently are

9) Future Close- set up a date for a future closing

10) Give Take Close- give them something then take it away

11) IQ close- product is a smart choice

12) Negative close- stress the disadvantages of failing to act on this

13) No Hassle Close- make it as easy as possible

14) Loss Opportunity Cost- show them the cost of not buying and loss of an opportunity
15) Rational Close- use logic and reasoning to get them to move forward
16) Shopping list close- list all their needs that the product or services addresses
17) Similarity Close- bond them to a person that was in a similar situation
18) Testimonial close- use a happy customer story
19) Think about it close- give them time to think- not too much time though
20) Trial close- pitch them closing before actual closing to see if they are ready

Appendix B: Mock Daily Schedule:

8:00AM- Get into work and organize yourself for the day

9:00 AM- email/call your follow-up leads

10:00AM- Work on current business and clients. Follow-up on documents, follow-up on stipulations, Follow-up on potential incoming packages

12PM- Solicit new business until lunch

1PM- Take lunch and clear head

2PM- answer e-mails and call backs for the day

3PM- Solicit for new business if time permits . Do outbound calls.

4PM- Make your hit list for tomorrow's follow-ups

Appendix C: 3 Call Sales Approach:

1) First Call- Determine the need, build rapport and determine their ROI (Return on Investment. Explain your product and get an application. Train to gain commitment by taking application over phone and having them sign.

2) Second Call- Reconfirm what they need. Earn more of a commitment and address their concerns about your product or service. Make sure your product and service helps them and fills a need. Conduct a trial close. See if they are ready to sign.

3) Third call- Present the full terms and details of contract and or loan. Assume the sale and gain their acceptance. Explain the final closing steps . Make sure everyone is on the same page. Review all documentation and have them sign while you are on the phone. Set full expectation and time frame and make sure this is it for borrower and they aren't shopping.

Appendix D: Best Practices Learned in Business Loan Selling:

1) Successful Calls:
   a. Confident in your approach and what you are saying
   b. Positive and Upbeat Energy
   c. Annunciation- Clear and Clarify what you are saying
   d. Tempo- not too fast but make sure you don't drag on
2) Set the tone- Make the merchant/customer feel like you should be the only person they need to talk to as they will be solicited by other organizations
3) Daily Agenda: set a schedule for yourself and get into a practice of following that daily.
4) Do not sell the borrower, consult them
   a. Your job is to put offers in from of the borrower that makes sense.
   b. Have them take you through their business model. How do they generate revenue? What is their sales cycle? How long does it take for them to complete a job to get paid? What are their profit

margins? The more you ask about their business the more ammunition you have to sell a product or loan offer.

Appendix E: Commission Breakdown Excel:

Deal Size	February % To Company	Commission to Company	My Split	My $		
$ 25,000.00	5%	$ 1,250.00	50%	$ 625.00		
$ 30,000.00	5%	$ 1,500.00	50%	$ 750.00		
$ 15,000.00	5%	$ 750.00	50%	$ 375.00		
$ 50,000.00	5%	$ 2,500.00	50%	$1,250.00		
				$3,000.00	Total	
				$6,000.00	Goal Per Month	
				50% off of My Target		

Appendix F: Snap Shot of Organized Email Folders-

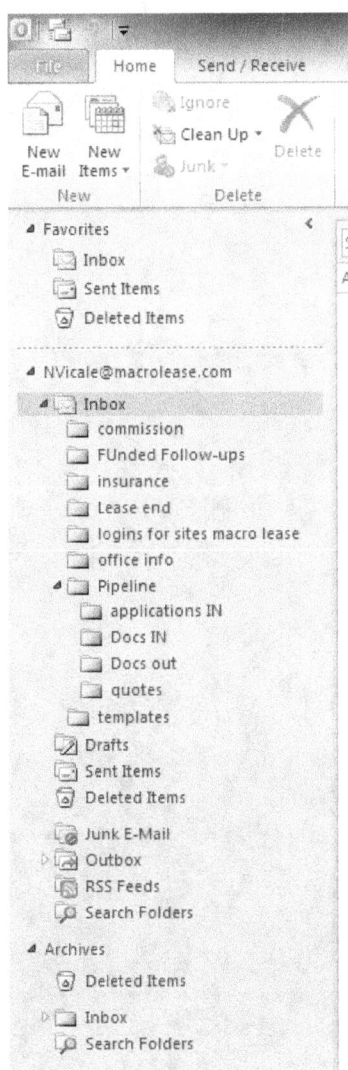

www.ingramcontent.com/pod-product-compliance
Lightning Source LLC
Chambersburg PA
CBHW070958240526
45469CB00017B/2451